NEW HAVEN FREE PUBLIC LIBRARY

3 5000 09583 512

P9-ARR-950

35000095835129

OFFICIALLY WITHDRAWN
NEW HAVEN FREE PUBLIC LIBRARY

364.106 BYERS
Frequently asked questions about
 gangs and urban violence /
35000095835129
MAIN LIBRARY

TEEN LIFE™

FREQUENTLY ASKED QUESTIONS ABOUT

Gangs and Urban Violence

Ann
Byers

ROSEN
PUBLISHING®

New York

Published in 2011 by The Rosen Publishing Group, Inc.
29 East 21st Street, New York, NY 10010

Copyright © 2011 by The Rosen Publishing Group, Inc.

First Edition

All rights reserved. No part of this book may be reproduced in any form without permission in writing from the publisher, except by a reviewer.

Library of Congress Cataloging-in-Publication Data

Byers, Ann.
Frequently asked questions about gangs and urban violence / Ann Byers.
    p. cm.—(FAQ: teen life)
Includes bibliographical references and index.
ISBN 978-1-4488-1325-4 (library binding)
1. Gangs—United States—Juvenile literature. 2. Urban violence—United States—Juvenile literature. I. Title.
HV6439.U5B94 2011
364.106'60973—dc22

                                                    2010014523

Manufactured in the United States of America

CPSIA Compliance Information: Batch #W11YA: For further information, contact Rosen Publishing, New York, New York, at 1-800-237-9932.

Contents

WHAT IS A GANG?
ARE THERE
DIFFERENT TYPES?

The Shirttails, the Plug Uglies, and the Dead Rabbits. These were the names of some of the biggest gangs of early nineteenth-century America. Today's gangs have more violent monikers: Men of Destruction, Shotgun Crips, and Murder Squad.

Young people have always liked to hang together in groups. Sometimes they just have fun, and sometimes they cause trouble. When people talk about a gang, they usually mean a group of three or more people who:

- Are together regularly and often
- Identify themselves by a common name and symbols
- See themselves as a gang and are recognized by others as a gang

- Are "street-oriented," which means their activities as a group are not done at home but on the streets or at other public places
- Are engaged in criminal activities

Being involved in criminal activities is what sets a group apart as a gang. Some of the crimes are fairly minor, like damaging property, stealing, or spraying graffiti. Some are more serious, like auto theft, assault, or dealing in drugs. All of them can get people in trouble.

Three Kinds of Gangs

The Federal Bureau of Investigation (FBI) lists three types of gangs that cause serious problems. One is the outlaw motorcycle gang. These gangs are not motorcycle clubs but highly organized, extremely violent groups of adults who buy and sell guns and drugs. They are a big problem for law enforcement but not for most citizens; their violence is usually aimed at people directly involved in their criminal activities.

The second type of gang is the prison gang. As the name implies, these are networks of men in prisons. Many were in street gangs and were arrested and sentenced to prison for the crimes they committed in those gangs. They cannot directly harm ordinary citizens, but they do pose an indirect threat. While in prison, they recruit and train new members for their gangs. They also sometimes give orders to their gang friends "on the outside," and those friends commit crimes in their

A police officer arrests two members of a motorcycle gang after a fight broke out during a motorcycle rally. Members of two rival gangs attacked one another with guns and knives, leaving some dead and wounded.

neighborhoods. Furthermore, when they have finished serving their sentences, they almost always return to their gangs.

By far the biggest problem for police—and for everyone else—is the street gang. There are far more street gangs than any other type and many, many more people in street gangs than in outlaw motorcycle and prison gangs. Street gangs can be found in practically every city in the country and in many rural areas. Their members are on the streets and in the parks, schools, and jails of their communities.

Street Gangs

Traditional street gangs are groups of young people, mostly males, who live near each other. They are also called "neighborhood gangs." They claim a certain turf, or geographic area, like a city block or set of blocks, as belonging to them. The main concern of turf-based gang members is controlling and defending their territory. They often pick fights with members of other gangs.

Turf gangs frequently evolve into gain-based gangs. These are groups that commit crimes for economic gain. They are usually involved in theft, robbery, or drug trafficking (buying and selling). The vast majority of gain-based gangs deal in drugs.

Turf-based gangs and drug gangs may look very similar, but there are some differences. Both groups commit a variety of crimes, but the crimes of turf-based gangs generally are against people in other gangs. Drug gangs commit more violent crimes against more people. Turf-based gangs compete for control of certain neighborhoods or blocks; drug gangs compete for control of the market for their goods. Turf-based gangs tend to have younger members and be more laid-back; drug gangs have older members and are deadly serious about what they do.

Some gangs are primarily or exclusively of one ethnic or racial group. That is because the neighborhood where they are located is made up mostly of one group. There are black gangs,

Filipino gang members are hanging out in Long Beach, California. Note the gun in one member's waistband. The oldest Filipino gang, the Santanas, began in the 1960s as a youth protection organization.

white gangs, Hispanic gangs, and Asian gangs in black, white, Hispanic, and Asian neighborhoods.

Many small street gangs want to tie themselves to larger, more well-known groups. They adopt their symbols and terms and call themselves "sets" or "cliques" of the bigger gangs. Members are called (collectively) a crew or a posse and (individually) gangbangers, bangers, homeboys, or homeys. Those who have pledged their allegiance form the core. Of these, the "hardcore" become leaders; they are the "shot callers." Most gangs have people who are on the fringe, who are involved in some of the gang's activities but have not completely bought in. They are

Boys who want to be part of a gang beat up a boy on the street as part of an initiation. To be admitted to the gang, they have to prove they are "tough" and will follow the orders of the leader.

ripe for recruitment for full-fledged membership. "Wannabes" are usually younger kids in the neighborhood who want in; if they hang around long enough, they might be able to join.

The Three Rs

The most important features of gang culture are the three Rs: reputation, respect, and retaliation. Reputation has to do with how people see the gang and its members. Members earn a good "rep" for themselves and their gang by being good at what the gang values. Usually that means fighting. Gangs want to be seen as tough. Members increase their reputation, also called "juice" and "street cred" (meaning credibility on the street), by beating up rivals, stealing cars or committing other crimes, and being sent to jail or juvenile hall.

The higher a gang's or a gang member's reputation, the greater respect they think they deserve. Gang members demand respect from all their homeys, force respect from other gangs through threats, and try to intimidate the community into respecting them. The "respect" is usually not admiration, but fear. Respect is so important to a banger that if someone disrespects, or "disses," his gang and one of his crew sees it and does nothing, that homey is punished.

Any disrespect brings retaliation. One of the strongest rules of gang life is that no act goes unanswered. Every offense, no matter how small, is met with revenge. Gang members do not only get even, they one-up someone who disrespects them. The slightest disagreement can quickly escalate into a beating or a gang fight. At one time, most gang retaliation stayed within the gangs and their families. Today, however, guns and cars have widened the reach of gangs.

Myths and Facts

 Gangs are a problem only in the run-down parts of large cities.
Fact ➡ Gangs are in big cities, small towns, and rural areas.

 Gangs are made up almost entirely of boys; girls in gangs are only girlfriends of the real gangsters.
Fact ➡ Male gang members far outnumber females, but many gangs do have female members. In fact, there are some all-girl gangs.

 Once a person is in a gang, that person is forever in the gang.
Fact ➡ With rare exceptions, people can get out of gangs as easily as they got in.

HOW BIG IS THE GANG PROBLEM?

Throughout history, when conditions were right, groups of young people have caused trouble. In the early 1800s, the Little Forty Thieves, a youth gang with members as young as ten, roamed inner-city neighborhoods in New York. There have always been gangs, but gangs have never been as big a problem as they are today, partly because of the use of guns and automobiles.

History of Gangs in the United States

One of the conditions that give rise to gangs is social instability. When everything is changing, young people look for something solid. They want to bring some sense of control and safety to the chaos around them. In a gang, they find security.

Al Capone, the gangster known as Scarface, was involved in illegally selling alcohol, gambling, prostitution, bribery, and murder. As this mug shot shows, he was finally arrested for "violating income tax laws" and sentenced to ten years in prison.

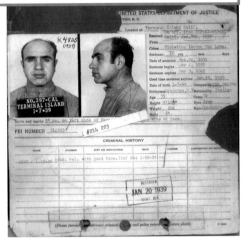

The 1800s was a period of great turmoil. The Industrial Revolution had caused people to move from the countryside to the cities. They gave up farming and went to work in factories. At the same time, immigrants from many countries poured into New York, Boston, Philadelphia, and other cities. Families packed into overcrowded apartments, competing for jobs and living space. The 1800s was a period of major gang growth in the United States.

At that time, most gangs were made up of people from the same ethnic group and nationality. Most were new arrivals who were trying to find their place in a strange environment: Irish, Italian, and Chinese immigrants. They began as bands of young men seeking protection and something to do. Most of what they did consisted of minor property crimes. As more positive opportunities opened up for them, gang activity declined.

A second period of gang growth began in the 1920s. Like the 1800s, this was a time of major social transition. It followed an economic depression and a world war. Often called the

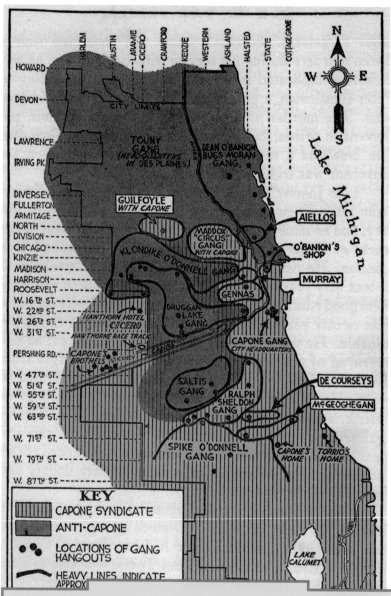

This map of a portion of Chicago around 1925 illustrates that Al Capone's organization controlled the city's South Side. The home indicated in the southeast section belonged to Johnny Torrio, the crime boss from whose territory Capone took over.

Golden Era of Gangs, the Roaring Twenties saw the birth of the Italian Mafia. Gangsters such as Al Capone and John Dillinger made headlines, and Chicago, Illinois, became the gang capital of the country. At the same time, youth gangs were also selling illegal alcohol and fighting one another for control of the alcohol trade. They became the recruiting ground for the "big leagues" of organized crime. Before moving to Chicago, Capone actually got his start in the James Street Gang, a youth gang in New York.

During the 1940s and 1950s, following World War II, America's cities were again in transition. Soldiers were returning from the battlefields, and more people were moving to urban centers in search of work. In low-income neighborhoods, people tended to cluster together in ethnic ghettos, defined by race. Young people in these areas banded together to defend themselves against real or imagined threats. They were mainly involved in turf wars, each gang trying to exert control over certain territory. The biggest groups were in Chicago: a Puerto Rican gang called the Latin Kings and the African American Vice Lords. In the Southwest, Mexican Americans began to form gangs.

The steadily growing gang activity exploded during the turbulent 1960s. America was rocked by the civil rights movement, the Vietnam War, and riots on college campuses. Some gangs, such as the Blackstone Rangers, began at that time as community organizations and eventually evolved into street gangs and then into criminal enterprises. The gang lifestyle was somewhat glamorized by the 1957 Broadway musical and 1961 movie

A Detroit police officer who specializes in narcotics has just hand-cuffed and arrested two youths on suspicion of dealing drugs. The officer is examining money he found in the youths' possession.

West Side Story. In the 1960s and 1970s, ethnic gangs grew larger and more violent. In New York, young people calling themselves by such names as the Savage Skulls and the Savage Nomads fought for dominance of the same streets. The Black P. Stone Rangers, the Devil's Disciples, and the Black Gangsters terrorized neighborhoods on Chicago's South Side. In Los Angeles, California, a gang called the Bloods arose to challenge the Crips.

Until the 1980s, the youth gangs were turf-based, defending their territories and challenging rival gang members. But in the mid-1980s, drugs came to U.S. cities in a big way. Crack cocaine was available at somewhat affordable prices. The country was again in a period of social upheaval. People working in factories were losing their jobs as companies went high-tech. The organized crime rings recruited juvenile gang members to help them sell cocaine and other substances. The young people, with no work available to them, readily agreed. Thus, many of the turf-based gangs became involved with drugs. Although most were not actually gain-based gangs, dealing in an organized way, their members sometimes sold drugs, usually marijuana, to make money for themselves.

As gang activity expanded, gangs formed alliances, which they called nations. In California, Hispanics in prison organized themselves into two rival groups: the Mexican Mafia, whose members were mostly from Southern California, and Nuestra Familia, inmates from the northern part of the state. When the released prisoners went back to their homes, they called their various street gangs Sureños (meaning "southerners") and Norteños (northerners). The many cliques thus merged into two very large, very powerful alliances. The gangs in Chicago made a similar arrangement, dividing most of the street gangs into sets of the Folk Nation or the People Nation.

As the exploits of these large alliances were publicized, gangs throughout the country began identifying themselves with the famous names. Crip, Blood, Folk, and People Nation sets popped up all over the United States. They claimed allegiance to the larger groups and adopted their names, symbols, and behaviors.

Gangs in the Twenty-first Century

Today, youth gangs can be found in every state. Many associate themselves with one of the four major gangs: the Los Angeles-based Crips or Bloods or the Chicago-based Folks or Peoples. A National Youth Gang Survey conducted by the U.S. Office of Juvenile Justice and Delinquency Prevention in 2007 identified more than 27,000 youth gangs in the United States with 788,000 members.

Most of these are in large cities and suburban counties, but gangs are spreading rapidly into small towns and rural areas also. Several gangs have spread from their hoods into neighboring regions and other states. These are not the small street gangs that want to claim an association with something bigger. These are huge enterprises that have tentacles that stretch far beyond the local level; some have "branches" in other countries. They are involved in more than drug trafficking; they also commit assaults, robberies, auto thefts, carjackings, drive-by shootings, homicides, and other felonies.

The national-level gangs are black, white, Hispanic, and Asian. Many are mixed-race gangs. Black national gangs include the oldest African American gang (Vice Lords), the largest gang in the country (Gangster Disciples), and its rival, the Black P. Stones. These groups began in Chicago but operate today across the country in cities from New York to Los Angeles.

The two black gangs that began in Los Angeles, the Bloods and the Crips, have sets in more than forty states. Nationally, however, Bloods and Crips are more like kinds of gangs than

A police car drives by a street corner in Memphis, Tennessee, where members of a Vice Lords set meet regularly. The Vice Lords, a People Nation group, dress in black and red.

actual interrelated groups. The 1988 movie *Colors* popularized the symbols and the activities of these two competing gangs, and young people began copying them in their own neighborhoods. Many of the thousands of youth who call themselves Crips or Bloods are simply members of neighborhood gangs who have adopted the names and lifestyles they have seen in the theater, on television, and on the Internet.

The only white national gang is the Aryan Brotherhood. Its members are often called skinheads because they shave their heads. The Aryan Brotherhood is still mostly a prison gang, but members who are released engage in typical gang activities on the streets. It is sometimes thought of as a hate group, rather than a gang. However, the street gangs distribute cocaine, heroin, marijuana, and methamphetamine. The Aryan Brotherhood is a very violent gang.

Hispanic gangs are not limited to Chicago and the southwest. The Chicago-based Latin Kings have spread to more than thirty states. The 18th Street, originally a California gang made up of illegal immigrants from Mexico and Central America, now operates in twenty states. The Sureños and Norteños have branched out beyond California. One of the largest and most violent Hispanic gangs in the United States is Mara Salvatrucha, also known as MS-13. Begun by refugees from El Salvador who lived in Los Angeles, the gang is strong in a number of Central American countries, as well as in major U.S. cities from Los Angeles to New York and Washington, D.C.

Most of the Asian gangs in the country are made up of Southeast Asian men originally from Vietnam, Cambodia, and

Laos. As refugee immigrants thrust suddenly into a culture very foreign to them, they banded together. Eventually, some of the bands became violent gangs, involved in drug dealing, auto theft, and home invasions. The Asian Boyz fanned out from Southern California to fourteen states. By far the most fearsome is the Tiny Rascals Gang, with more than sixty sets throughout the entire country.

The large national gangs have tens of thousands of members, they make sensational headlines, and they drain law enforcement of much time and money. But most ordinary citizens have no contact with these groups. They are more concerned with the smaller, local gangs that are present on city streets and country roads, in large shopping malls and corner stores, and in many of our nation's public schools.

WHO JOINS A GANG?
WHY DO THEY JOIN?

Youth gang members are generally between the ages of ten and twenty-four; the average age is seventeen or eighteen. Typically, gang involvement is a three-step process: awareness, engagement, and enlistment. Every young person who lives in an area with gang activity is in one of the three stages. They all are aware of what is taking place around them. They know who the gang members are. By age twelve or thirteen, some adolescents become engaged with the gang in their neighborhood. They hang around members, watch what they do, and learn the rules. Somewhere between ages thirteen and fifteen, they are enlisted, and some become full-fledged members.

Their reasons for joining are varied. For many, being part of a gang gives a sense of self-worth, a feeling of belonging, acceptance, and status. For some, it gives protection. Others join for the excitement and adventure they think it offers, and others for a chance to make money. None of these motivations are bad; all are important in adolescent development. As children grow up, most find these things in a healthy family, a positive school experience, participation in sports and other wholesome activities, and jobs. However, some young people do not have these opportunities, and so they turn to gangs.

Community Factors

The community in which young people live determines what opportunities for healthy development they have. If the neighborhood is unstable, with people moving in and out, adolescents do not feel secure. They have no sense of belonging because whatever they belong to keeps changing. They have to keep working to gain acceptance because old friends leave and new people come. They have to prove themselves over and over.

If the area is a high-crime neighborhood, young people do not feel safe. They may see little choice but to join the group that seems to wield the most power. They think that belonging to the gang will protect them from threats coming into the neighborhood and keep gang members from bullying or harassing them. In schools in high-crime areas, members of rival gangs may be in the same classroom. Having fellow gang members nearby makes some students feel safe. Although young people may join a gang for self-protection, membership actually makes them less safe. It opens them to attacks from rival gangs.

Poor communities usually have little to offer young people in the way of opportunities. The schools in these neighborhoods are often below standard, and chances for employment are low. On the other hand, criminal opportunities may be readily available. Selling drugs, grabbing a purse, or stealing a car may be the only avenues a young person sees for making any money. Many poor communities do not have bowling alleys, movie theaters, nice parks, or other forms of affordable recreation. Gang action presents some excitement in a dull, drab neighborhood.

The way young people in the community look at gangs plays a role in whether someone wants to join one. If relatives and schoolmates view gang membership as something good or something expected, young people will be drawn in. Media portrayals of gang lifestyles are attractive to many youths. Movies, video games, magazines, certain music, and some Web sites paint gang life as full of bravado, adventure, wealth, and

A graffiti expert examines writing on a wall in Springfield, Massachusetts. The graffiti contains symbols used by the Folk Nation gangs and the Gangster Disciple Nation.

reputation—all qualities young people want but are often out of their reach.

Thus, communities that are poor, unstable, and crime-ridden—communities in which gang life is glorified—are breeding grounds for street gangs.

Personal Factors

Every young person in such communities does not join a gang, and some people in wealthy communities do. Personal factors also comes into play. Young people need to feel self-worth, belonging, acceptance, and achievement to make a successful transition to adulthood. Those who lack these important characteristics are particularly vulnerable to the lure of gangs.

A sense of self-worth, belonging, and acceptance usually come from healthy relationships. Some young people grow up in unhealthy settings: without a father, with abusive adults, in violent homes, or with parents who do not pay them any attention. They have little or no love, structure, or discipline. They do not feel they are valued. They may turn to others in similar situations to belong to something. For some, a gang is the closest thing they have to what a family should be. One of the oldest Hispanic prison gangs still calls itself Nuestra Familia—Our Family. Homeys often call one another "bro," meaning brother.

A sense of value and acceptance also come from academic achievement. Young people who are not doing well in school tend to feel bad about themselves. Their low self-esteem makes gang life attractive. They can achieve success in a gang without

This is what remains of a dormitory in a men's prison in Chino, California, after a racially motivated riot. Nearly two hundred inmates were injured in the violence and the fire. Prison riots are frequently the result of arguments between rival gangs.

studying and taking tests. They do not have to have good grades to steal a car.

Certain behaviors make a young person open to gang membership. People who use alcohol, marijuana, or other drugs tend to gravitate toward gangs. These substances are readily available in most gang circles today. So are money, sex, and wild times. Adolescents who value these "benefits" are drawn to gangs.

The type of people in a child's life can greatly influence that child's likelihood of being enlisted into a gang. Children who are closely supervised by caring adults have an easier time resisting the temptations of gangs. On the other hand, children whose role models are violent are likely to imitate their heroes. Young people whose friends and relatives are delinquent or in gangs will probably follow their example.

Some children are "born into" gangs. Their fathers and perhaps their grandfathers were gang members. These children learn the gang culture early and are expected to continue the family tradition.

Racial/Ethnic Factor

Most modern gangs began as racial or ethnic groupings, and many appear to remain so today. However, gangs do not always have a hard and fast rule about the race of their members. Generally, the racial makeup of a gang reflects the larger community in which the gang is located. In other words, gangs in African American neighborhoods are predominantly African

American, gangs in Hispanic neighborhoods are mostly Hispanic, and gangs in white neighborhoods are largely white.

Many inner-city areas of major cities in the United States consist largely of minorities. Therefore, urban gangs are primarily African American and Hispanic. In smaller cities and rural areas, however, where the population is mainly Caucasian, there are often white gangs. In fact, the number of white gangs in these neighborhoods is on the rise. The number of Asian gangs is smaller because Asians make up a small percentage of the total population.

Females in Gangs

Males outnumber females in street gangs by at least ten to one. Although gangs are largely "boys clubs," they have always had girls around. Often the girls are "hangers-on"—relatives and girlfriends of gang members. Sometimes they are involved in the less violent activities of the gang: carrying weapons, drugs, and information. Some attach themselves to the gangs for the partying, the drugs, and the sex; gangbangers call these girls "hood rats."

In some gangs, however, girls have gained respect as members in good standing. There are some all-girl gangs. Most of these are cliques or sets of male gangs. For example, the Varrio Locas are a female version of the Varrio Locos. Cripettes and Bloodettes identify themselves with the Los Angeles-based male gangs. Playgirl Sureñas hang out with male Sureños. The Latin Queens gang is part of the Almighty Latin King and Queen Nation.

These girls belong to one of the nearly twenty sets of Maravilla gangs in East Los Angeles. The Maravilla (Spanish for "marvelous") gangs broke away from the Sureños, and the two are now enemies.

Girls join gangs for the same reasons boys do. Some are trying to escape what they see as abusive situations at home. Others are simply rebelling against their parents. Some are looking for protection, and some think gang life will be fun. Girls do not tend to stay in gangs as long as boys; they often become pregnant and drop out to care for their children.

Gang Recruitment

In the very small number of street gangs that are criminal enterprises, gang leaders want to expand their "businesses."

They are constantly losing "employees" to prison and street violence, so they must continually recruit new members. Unlike lawful employers, they do not look for people with skills and experience. They want people who are young and easily swayed. The best age for new recruits is between the ages of eleven and thirteen.

Young people have advantages in the crime business. First, police officers may watch known gang members, but they may not suspect that a twelve-year-old is carrying drugs. Second, police and judges are likely to "go softer" on young offenders. A sixteen-year-old may be tried as an adult and imprisoned for beating and robbing someone, but his younger brother will probably be let off with a warning. The gang may place a potential member as young as nine as a lookout or a messenger boy and gradually move him up to more responsible assignments.

In the vast majority of street gangs, members are not recruited; young people want to join. Many are lured by their idea of gang culture. Bangers tell stories that portray their lives as confident and adventurous. They show off their cars and their jewelry, their girls, and their crews. They make their wounds and close calls seem like heroic medals. Young people are drawn in by the mystique of the gang's symbols, the fun of their parties, and the brotherhood of their members.

But like shiny lures on a barbed fishhook, the picture is not completely true. The stories are usually exaggerated, the material goods do not last long, and the fights all too often end in tragedy.

Older gang members can spot young people who are likely to join them. They watch for those who go home from school to empty houses, for those with no one to supervise them and nothing to do. They listen to hear who is struggling in school. They pick out loners and try to convince them that their group is a friendly club of people who look out for one another.

Sometimes members will threaten potential recruits. They might harass them and then promise protection. They may do something for them—give them money or get them out of trouble—and expect them to join the gang to pay them back. They will use pressure from older peers. They may tell them there is no safety outside the gang, and they might use force to convince them.

Many young people do not need threats. These "wannabes" hang around their older brothers, cousins, and friends and look for ways to prove their worth. Eventually, they make it in.

four

WHAT KINDS OF ACTIVITIES ARE GANGS INVOLVED IN?

Gang members, whether in the city or country, spend their time in three types of activities: maintaining the gang's presence in the community, defending their reputation and their territory, and making money.

A gang first makes its presence known by its name. Often the name tells where the gang is located: the Weller boys are on Weller Street; the Fink Whites are around the Fink White Park; there is a 2300 Lotus gang and a 2400 Lotus gang on two different blocks of the same street. In St. Louis, Missouri, the 49 BAD Bloods claim the 4900 blocks of Beacon, Alcott, and Davison avenues. Members who want to identify themselves with a well-known gang add its name to their own: the Denver Lane Bloods, the Carver Park Compton Crips.

The way gangs advertise their presence in a neighborhood is through the use of colors, numbers, and symbols.

Colors and Clothes

Each gang chooses a particular color as its own. Bloods wear red, and their rivals, the Crips, wear blue. Norteños also use red, and their rivals, the Sureños, wear blue. Many of the Folk Nation and People Nation combine black with other colors. The Gangster Disciples wear black and blue, the Vice Lords black and red, and the Latin Kings black and gold. Mara Salvatrucha members use blue and white, the colors of the flag of El Salvador. Asian Boyz wear blue, whereas the Tiny Rascals sport gray.

Bangers wear, or "fly," these colors in a variety of ways. The old standby is the bandanna, also called a "rag," tied around the forehead or neck or hanging from the pocket or belt loop of pants. When it is on the head, it is known as a "durag" (also spelled "do-rag"). Gang members select clothing in their gang's color: hats, shirts, and shoes. When schools began to ban gang colors, members got creative; they switched to plain shoes tied with colored laces. When those were also forbidden, they put colored beads on their shoe laces. Beads in gang colors now also appear in necklaces and wristbands, on key chains, and in hair braids.

Gang members use colors to communicate to their gangs and their rivals, but they may not want to advertise to their parents or school officials that they are banging. So they find subtle ways to

Following riots and beatings by police in Los Angeles in 1992, several large sets of the Bloods and Crips in that city declared a truce. Two former enemies display their colors in clutched hands to show they stand united against police brutality.

fly their colors. One source is sports clothing. The black and red of the Chicago Bulls is perfect for the Vice Lords, and the red of the San Francisco Forty-Niners fits the Norteños. Latin Kings like the black and gold of the Pittsburg Pirates, and Gangster Disciples wear the black and blue of the Detroit Tigers.

A bonus to some sports clothing is that the initials can be related to the gang. The BK in British Knight shoes can represent Blood Killer, and the CK on Calvin Klein shirts can refer to Crips Killer. The DB of Denver Broncos is a backward reading of Black Disciples. Latin Kings proudly wear L.A. Kings jerseys.

Some gang members wear their pants low on their hips; this is called "sagging." The practice might have originated from pictures the young people received from their relatives in prison. Prison officials usually took prisoner's belts away from them to prevent violence and suicides. In the pictures the prisoners took, their pants sagged, and the boys at home copied their heroes.

Young people who wear certain colors, like clothing from professional sports teams, or sag their pants are not necessarily in gangs. Hip-hop artists, rappers, and videos have made some of these styles popular with a lot of teens. However, innocent people have sometimes gotten hurt because gang members looking to pick fights with their rivals could not tell the difference between real gangbangers and look-alikes.

Numbers and Symbols

In addition to colors, gangs use numbers as a kind of code. Often numbers replace letters. Members of the Vice Lords sometimes

write the gang name as 2212; 22 is for V, the twenty-second letter of the alphabet, and 12 is for L. A Black Gangster Disciple is
a 274, code for BGD. Sureños use the number 13 to represent the
letter M; it stands for the initials of its parent gang, the Mexican
Mafia. Norteños use 14 in place of N, for Nuestra Familia.
Sureños may write the number as 13, XIII, or X3, or they may
simply use three dots. Likewise, Norteños identify themselves as
14, XIV, X4, or with four dots. Mara Salvatrucha goes by MS-13,
placing the number 13 after the gang's initials because it was
formed in Southern California, Sureño territory. The Tiny
Rascals Gang uses the number 7126 because the numbers can
be written in a way to look like the initials TRG.

Gangs also adopt certain symbols that distinguish them from
others and link them to the groups with which they are associated. People Nation gangs use symbols that originated with the
Vice Lords, one of the founding gangs. Considering themselves
lords, the early members used as their symbols a crown, a top
hat and cane, and a martini glass. Gangs in the People Nation
also draw a star, a star and crescent, a die (one of a pair of dice),
and a bunny head. They identify with the number five, so the
crown and the star each has five points, and the die has five dots.
Rival gangs of the Folk Nation use the number six. They have a
star with six points and a die with six dots. In contrast to the cane
of the People Nation, Folk Nation gangs have adopted a pitch-
fork. They also use a bunny, but one ear is bent down. Individual
sets use these and additional symbols.

The colors, numbers, and symbols have to be displayed in the
right way. They are hung in windows, drawn on backpacks, and

Members of the Pico Norte 19th Street gang in El Paso, Texas, flash their hand signs and show their tattoos. Nineteen signifies the name of the gang, fourteen indicates that they are Norteños, and the three dots stand for *mi vida loca* ("my crazy life").

painted on fences. They might be shaved on someone's head. Many gangbangers tattoo them permanently on their chests, backs, arms, necks, hands, and faces.

People Nation groups have decided that they will identify to the left. That is, they will do as much as they can toward the left side of their bodies. So a member of the Black P. Stones, for example, will tilt the bill of his cap or the buckle of his belt to the left. He might roll up his left pant leg or his left shirt sleeve, untie his left shoe, or pull the tongue of one shoe out. He could wear jewelry on his left arm, an earring in his left ear, and a glove only on his left hand. He might make a point of putting his left hand in his pocket. A member of a Folk Nation group will do all these to the right. Moreover, members will throw their gang signs to the appropriate side.

Throwing Signs

Throwing hand signs is an important way for a gang member to show what gang he is with. Gangsters form the initials, numbers, or symbols of their gangs with their fingers. They display, or "throw" or "flash," the sign either to identify themselves to friends or to challenge foes. Different sets of the same gang may have their own signs. Some signs are very simple initials. A Crip may make a C with his hand. A Sureño joins two Cs to form an S. Vice Lords raise the first two fingers and the thumb to form the letters V and L.

Some signs represent a gang's number. A Norteño clique may use a one and a four or simply a four, and a Sureño clique might use a three. Some Bloods can arrange their fingers to spell out the entire word "Blood." Signs can also depict a gang's symbols. Latin Kings use both hands to make a five-pointed star and Black Gangster Disciples make a winged heart. The raised index and little finger signify a devil's head to an MS-13 member, and turned upside down, the devil's head looks like the letter M.

Gang members know that police can easily identify them when they are flying their colors. But they can flash a sign when a police officer turns his or her head. Some are wearing their colors less and throwing their signs more.

Graffiti

Gangs establish and defend themselves in a community with graffiti. Graffiti consists of gang messages scrawled on walls, fences, or any other public place. Graffiti has been called the newspaper or the bulletin board of the street. It is used to proclaim a gang's presence in a neighborhood, mark its territory, boast about any of its victories, and announce some of its next

A member of the Playboys gang tags a building in Los Angeles. He is marking his turf, warning other gangs to stay out of the neighborhood. The initials P and B stand for Playboy, and the S indicates it is a Sureño gang.

moves. Most gang graffiti has the name, number, or a symbol of the gang. Sometimes it has the moniker of a particular gangster, and often it has a coded message.

The coded message is frequently a way to dis rivals or threaten them. Drawing a gang's symbol upside down, for example, is a direct challenge. A Blood will substitute a B for every C in the message to disrespect Crips. Crips will find a Blood's message and cross out every B. Usually when something is crossed out, one gang is threatening another. If the letter K appears after the name of a gang or a person, the writer is saying he is planning to kill someone. In California, the number 187 in graffiti delivers the same message; 187 is the penal code number for homicide. Similarly, when the number 211 is in the graffiti, the gang is warning that a robbery is about to be committed. Certain terms are put-downs of specific gangs: crab, slob, scrap, and buster. When these words show up in graffiti, one gang is dissing another and asking for a fight.

Graffiti should not be confused with tagging. Taggers use spray paint to post messages also, but their messages are generally only their names and sometimes the name of a gang they might be loosely associated with. Taggers consider themselves artists, and their goal is to see their names in as many places as possible. They are especially happy if they can spray their name on hard-to-reach spots such as freeway overpasses. Real gangbangers do not consider tagging crews actual gangs. Neither do police because they are not involved in crimes any more serious than vandalism. However, tagging crews sometimes develop into more serious gangs.

Getting In and Getting Out

How does someone begin gang life? He has to be accepted into the brotherhood. Most gangs have initiation rituals. The most common is some form of "jumping in." The prospective member is "jumped," or beaten, by gang members for a set period of time, usually less than a minute. For MS-13, it is for thirteen seconds; for its rival, 18th Street, it is eighteen seconds. A variation of this ritual is "lining in." In this initiation, the new member must walk between two lines of members beating on him. These rites give the new banger a chance to prove how tough he is.

Criminal gangs sometimes recruit a person who has a specific skill or connection. He might be good at carjacking, or he might have a great source for guns or drugs. This person might be "courted in." That is, he is simply invited to join. In gangs that accept females, girls are sometimes "sexed in." They are required to have sex with one or more gang members. In some gangs that specialize in a particular type of crime, prospective members must prove their skill by successfully committing that crime. They may have to steal a car, break into a home, or even kill someone.

How does someone get out of a gang? Many people "age out"—they get too old to want to stay involved. Often they just stop hanging around. Unless they are hard-core, most gang-bangers stay in a gang for less than a year. In gangs in which people are jumped in, they may have to be jumped out. Only a very, very few gangs—mostly prison gangs—enforce a "blood in, blood out" rule, meaning a person cannot leave a gang alive. Some gangs talk about this rule to reinforce loyalty to the group, but when people do leave, the other gang members do not bother them. Some of their rivals may still be after them, and some former gang members have had to move to get away from the enemies they made while in the gang.

Crime

Most street gangs are not criminal gangs, but many members of street gangs commit crimes. That is, the majority of neighbor-hood gangs are not organized groups that burglarize homes, steal cars, or deal drugs to make money for the gang. However, members of those gangs may commit these and other crimes to get money for themselves. Sometimes, street gangs appear to be criminal gangs specializing in certain types of unlawful activi-ties. For example, home invasions are very often thought to be

As an enforcer for the Gangster Disciples, Wallace "Gator" Bradley served a four-year jail term for armed robbery. Fifteen years later, as a community organizer, he campaigned unsuccessfully to become a Chicago alderman. At this news conference, he distances himself from the Disciples.

the work of Southeast Asian gangs. The truth is that many of the invasions or other crimes are not ordered and carried out by the gang, but the project of a few gangbangers. Their homeys see their success and learn their techniques, and before long others in the same gang are committing the same crime.

Gang members commit crimes for several reasons. Sometimes they assault members of rival gangs out of retaliation, to look good in front of others, or simply for sport. They might vandalize property or steal a car just for the excitement of it. When they deal in drugs, it is usually to make some quick money.

Part of the attraction of gang life lies in the "stuff" gang members own—"in" clothes, a hot car, the latest gadgets. Those things cost more money than many young people have. Because drug use is common in and around gangs, gang members often have access to drugs. Most street gang members do not sell drugs regularly, but when they are out of money, dealing drugs can get them what they want.

Ten Great Questions to Ask a Guidance Counselor

1 Does graffiti in my neighborhood mean that it is gang territory?

2 All my friends are in a gang and want me to join. How do I say no?

3 Once someone is in a gang, can he ever get out?

4 If someone is always wearing blue and his pants sag, does that mean he is in a gang?

5 I live in a rough neighborhood with gangs. Will joining a gang keep me safe?

6 If I go to an event that gang members might attend, is it dangerous for me to wear clothing with a professional sports team's logo?

7 If I see graffiti on my fence, should I paint over it right away?

8 My younger brother likes movies and music about gangs. What can I do to discourage him from becoming involved with a gang?

9 When I see students fighting after school, what should I do?

10 My friends and I think some of the gang symbols and signs we see on Web sites are cool. Is it OK if we use them just between us?

WHAT CAN BE DONE ABOUT GANGS AND GANG VIOLENCE?

Law enforcement and youth workers attack the problem of gangs in three ways: prevention, intervention, and suppression.

Prevention

The best way to stop gang violence is to keep young people from wanting to join. The first step in prevention is to make sure children have what they need so they do not turn to gangs. Children need the things a healthy family provides: love, guidance, supervision, and responsibilities. They need to belong and feel important. Children need a safe environment and activities that help them develop confidence. They need to learn how to get along with others. They need positive role models to show them how to become good adults. Gang prevention begins with parents and other adults making sure their children have these foundations.

But not all children have the basics they need. For them, adults in the community need to step in and fill the gaps. Teachers, coaches, and big brothers and sisters can provide some of what the children lack. Churches and community organizations can offer social activities and positive reinforcement. They can offer their members as mentors to youth. The more a community can create a positive family feel, the less attractive gang life will be.

However, some young people will be drawn to gangs despite the best efforts of the adults in their lives. Therefore, parents must be aware of any indication that their children may be interested in gangs. Prevention means stopping the activity at the very first sign. Some of the early signs of possible gang involvement are these:

- Negative changes in behavior, such as ditching school, getting lower grades, staying out late, being disrespectful, and being secretive
- Unusual interest in particular colors or symbols
- Interest in gang-type music, movies, or videos
- Practicing or using hand signals
- Unusual drawings or gang symbols on books, clothes, backpacks, or other items
- Dropping good friends and forming new friendships
- Use of alcohol or other substances
- Unexplained injuries that could come from fighting
- Unexplained possession of money or other items

Teens in Miami Beach, Florida, listen to a speaker at an antidrug event. The tattoos on the speaker's neck and hand suggest that he is a former gang member.

Spotting the signs takes intentional involvement in children's lives. It means talking with them and really listening, staying on top of their schoolwork, and getting to know their friends. The best time to stop gang activity is before it starts.

Intervention

If prevention fails and young people join gangs, the next step is intervention. In this step, adults intervene, or step in, to encourage individual young people to stop their involvement with gangs. It targets the youngest gang members and attempts to pull them away from the group. As with prevention, intervention is a matter of offering young people what they need. Adults

With the motto "Nothing stops a bullet like a job," Homeboy Industries in Los Angeles created a number of small businesses that train and employ young people who might otherwise be in gangs. These girls are preparing lunches in the Homegirl Café.

provide alternatives to what the gang offers, alternatives they hope will be more attractive.

One of the alternatives is wholesome recreational outlets. Boys and Girls Clubs and other after-school programs have fun activities with adult supervision. Sports leagues, boxing clubs, and drama groups can all give young people something to do, a chance to achieve, and a group to belong to. They also usually provide positive role models and motivation for socially acceptable behaviors.

To come away from gangs, young people need good educations that will prepare them for successful futures. They need the opportunity to find and get decent jobs. Many of the neighborhoods with the heaviest gang activity have poor schools and few, if any, employment opportunities. Intervention means improving the schools, providing job training, and giving young people extra help in locating, obtaining, and keeping jobs.

Intervention also means providing social services in those neighborhoods that lack them. Many of the young people who are drawn to gangs are surrounded by poverty, unhealthy conditions, alcohol and drugs, and violence. They become depressed or angry, and they give in to alcohol or drugs and become violent themselves. Until their environment can be changed, the young people need help to rise above it. Intervention means providing health care, counseling, tutoring, substance abuse treatment, and anger management programs.

Suppression

The best prevention and intervention efforts will not put hardcore gang members out of business. The final step in getting rid of the gang problem is suppression. Suppression is any measure that breaks up gangs and stops gang activity. Suppression efforts are all undertaken by law enforcement agencies.

Most police departments attempt to combat gangs through community-based policing. Officers work with individuals and organizations in their communities to identify problems and solve them. Police and citizens work together to maintain a safe community. Through Neighborhood Watch types of organizations, public meetings, and good communication, residents and police keep everyone informed about what is happening in their neighborhoods. If someone spots a problem, the citizens and police discuss ways to address it. Often, this cooperative approach is able to stop crimes before they occur.

When gang crimes do occur, suppression means that the people responsible, especially the older, hard-core gang members, are arrested. When the leaders are in juvenile hall, jail, or prison, the gang suffers. The Los Angeles County District Attorney's Office has a Hardcore Gang Division with more than fifty lawyers whose full-time jobs are making sure that the worst offenders stay behind bars once they are caught.

For the less serious gangbangers, the ones who are arrested, serve their time, and are back on the streets, suppression means close supervision. While these less-hardened gang members are on probation, they are watched carefully. If they are found associating with other gang members, they will find themselves back in prison.

One form of gang suppression that can involve the entire community is graffiti removal. When one graffiti message goes up, the three Rs of gang culture demand that a rival gang respond—with more graffiti and perhaps with violent action. Graffiti invites more graffiti; the longer it is up, the bigger it grows. An obvious way to reduce gang activity is to get rid of the graffiti. However, the writing may contain information that can help police deal with the larger problem. Therefore, law enforcement agencies ask citizens to follow the four Rs of graffiti removal:

1. Read it. You might be able to tell something about the gang, the members, and what they are planning to do.
2. Report it. Many police departments have special gang units trained to interpret the scrawls.

In a police department neighborhood cleanup program in San Fernando, California, gang members who have been caught writing graffiti paint over it while officers supervise from their parked patrol car.

3. Record it. Take a picture of it in case the police need the details later.

4. Remove it right away. Special graffiti removal products are available, but the best way to get rid of it is to paint over it. Don't paint just the spot; paint the whole wall or whatever object the graffiti is written on.

Gangs have become a very big problem everywhere in the country. But most young people do not join gangs. Most of those who do join do not stay in for long. Besides, most citizens do not want gangs in their communities. That means that no matter how big the problem is, it can be overcome.

bang To be a member of a gang involved in gang activities. A gang member is a banger or a gangbanger.

bravado Boldness, boasting, or bragging.

clique A gang, usually modeling itself after one of the larger gangs.

crew Members of a gang.

delinquent Antisocial or unlawful; someone, especially a young person, who has acted antisocially or has broken the law.

dis Abbreviation for the word "disrespect."

durag Pronounced "doo-rag," a bandanna or handkerchief in a gang's color tied around a member's head.

extort To obtain money through force or threats.

hood A neighborhood or other area claimed by a gang.

hood rat A girl who hangs out with a gang but is not really part of it.

juvenile hall A detention center for young people, usually a secure residential facility.

moniker A name.

penal code Section of a state's laws that gives a number to each type of crime.

posse Members of a gang.

probation The supervision of the behavior of a young or first-time criminal offender by a probation officer.

During the time of supervision, the offender must routinely report to the probation officer and must not commit any further offenses.

rag A handkerchief or bandanna in a gang's color.

rep A gang term for "reputation."

sagging Wearing one's pants low on the hips, usually with underwear (often of a gang color) showing above the pants' waistline.

set A gang, usually modeling itself after one of the larger gangs.

street cred One's reputation in the neighborhood, or credibility on the streets.

trafficking Buying and selling; dealing.

turf Originally, a plot of grass. Now used to refer to a geographic area, such as a neighborhood.

vandalism The purposeful destruction of property.

wannabe A person who is not yet a gang member but wants to be one.

Gang Prevention: A Resource Guide on Youth and Gangs
Produced by the Nova Scotia Department of Justice,
Canada Department of Justice
Web site: http://www.gov.ns.ca/just/publications/
documents/GangPrevention.pdf
This guide provides easy-to-read information for youth,
parents, teachers, and others on gang development,
operation, and prevention. It contains very comprehensive and practical information.

National Crime Prevention Centre of Public Safety, Canada
269 Laurier Avenue West
Ottawa, ON K1A 0P8
Canada
(877) 302-6272
Web site: http://www.publicsafety.gc.ca
This agency of the Canadian government develops
and distributes information about youth gangs
in Canada.

National Drug Intelligence Center
319 Washington Street, Fifth Floor
Johnstown, PA 15901-1622
(814) 532-4601

Web site: http://www.justice.gov/ndic

This center provides news and information about the production, transportation, distribution, and abuse of illegal drugs. It also charts trends of drug trafficking organizations and street gangs.

National Gang Center

Institute for Intergovernmental Research

P.O. Box 12729

Tallahassee, FL 32317

(850) 385-0600

Web site: http://www.nationalgangcenter.gov

The National Gang Center provides the latest research and most up-to-date resources on gangs and antigang programs.

National Gang Intelligence Center

935 Pennsylvania Avenue NW

NGIC-VA-#405

Washington, DC 20535

(800) 366-9501

Web site: http://www.justice.gov/ngic

A partnership of several federal, state, and local agencies, the National Gang Intelligence Center gathers and makes available information on gangs that operate at the national and regional levels.

National School Safety and Security Services

P.O. Box 110123

Cleveland, OH 44111

(216) 251-3067

Web site: http://www.schoolsecurity.org/trends/gangs.html

National School Safety and Security Services is a national
consulting company providing information and training in
safety for elementary through high schools. Its Web site
has information on gangs in general and managing and
preventing gangs in school.

Web Sites

Due to the changing nature of Internet links, Rosen Publishing
has developed an online list of Web sites related to the subject
of this book. This site is updated regularly. Please use this link to
access the list:

http://www.rosenlinks.com/faq/gang

Brown, Don. *The Notorious Izzy Fink*. New York, NY: Roaring Brook Press, 2006.

Corbett, David. *Do They Know I'm Running?* New York, NY: Ballantine, 2010.

Davis, Sampson, George Jenkins, Sharon Draper, and Rameck Hunt. *We Beat the Street: How a Friendship Pact Led to Success*. New York, NY: Penguin, 2006.

Draper, Sharon M. *Battle of Jericho*. New York, NY: Simon and Schuster, 2005.

Duffy, Maureen P., and Scott Edward Gillig, eds. *Teen Gangs: A Global View*. Westport, CT: Greenwood, 2004.

Hamilton, Jill. *Gangs*. San Diego, CA: Greenhaven, 2007.

Newton, Michael. *Gangs and Gang Crimes* (Criminal Investigations). New York, NY: Chelsea House Publishers, 2008.

Venkatesh, Sudhir. *Gang Leader for a Day: A Rogue Sociologist Takes to the Streets*. New York, NY: Penguin, 2008.

Asbury, Herbert. *The Gangs of New York: An Informal History of the Underworld*. New York, NY: Random House, 2008.

Egley, Arlen, Jr., and Christina E. O'Donnell. *Highlights of the 2007 National Youth Gang Survey* (OJJDP Fact Sheet). Washington, DC: U.S. Department of Justice, Office of Justice Programs, Office of Juvenile Justice and Delinquency Prevention, 2006. Retrieved April 29, 2010 (http://www.ncjrs.gov/pdffiles1/ojjdp/225185.pdf).

Garrison, Chad. "Battle Lines." *St. Louis Riverfront Times*, August 23, 2006. Retrieved March 30, 2010 (http://www.riverfronttimes.com/2006-08-23/news/battle-lines).

Greene, Judith, and Kevin Pranis. *Gang Wars: The Failure of Enforcement Tactics and the Need for Effective Public Safety Strategies*. Washington, DC: Justice Policy Institute, 2007.

Howell, James C., and Scott H. Decker. "The Youth Gangs, Drugs, and Violence Connection." *Juvenile Justice Bulletin* (Report NCJ-171152). Washington, DC: U.S. Department of Justice, Office of Juvenile Justice and Delinquency Prevention, 1999.

Lewis, Jared. "The History of Gangs." *Know Gangs*. Retrieved March 29, 2010 (http://www.knowgangs.com/gang_resources/411/history/history2.php).

National Gang Intelligence Center. *National Gang Threat Assessment 2009*. Publication 2009-M0335-001. Washington, DC, 2009.

Snyder, Howard N., and Melissa Sickmund. *Juvenile Offenders and Victims: 2006 National Report*. Washington, DC: U.S. Department of Justice, Office of Justice Programs, Office of Juvenile Justice and Delinquency Prevention, 2006.

Urban Dynamics, Inc. *Comprehensive Community Reanimation Process*. Excerpts posted at Gangs 101. Retrieved March 28, 2010 (http://lincolnnet.net/users/lrttrapp/http/block/gangs101.htm).

About the Author

A youth worker with a national faith-based youth organization, Ann Byers has worked directly with a number of current and former young gang members.

Photo Credits

Cover, p. 35 © Mark Richards/PhotoEdit; pp. 6, 27, 44 © AP Images; p. 8 © Michael Newman/PhotoEdit; pp. 9, 53 © A. Ramey/Photo Edit; p. 13 FBI; p. 14 Chicago History Museum/ Getty Images; p. 16 John Chiasson/Getty Images; p. 19 Mike Brown/The Commercial Appeal/Landov; pp. 24–25 Chistopher Evans/The Republican/Landov; p. 30 Joe Rodriguez/Gallery Stock; pp. 38–39 Hector Mata/AFP/Getty Images; p. 41 Robert Yaeger/Stone/Getty Images; p. 49 © Jeff Greenberg/PhotoEdit; p. 50 Lucy Nicholson/Reuters/Landov.

Designer: Evelyn Horovicz; Editor: Kathy Kuhtz Campbell; Photo Researcher: Marty Levick